Local Visitations

Local Visitations

poems

Stephen Dunn

 W. W. Norton & Company New York London

For information about permission to reproduce selections from this book, write to Permissions, W. W. Norton & Company, Inc., 500 Fifth Avenue, New York, NY 10110

Manufacturing by The Courier Companies, Inc.
Book design by Chris Welch
Production manager: Anna Oler

LIBRARY OF CONGRESS CATALOGING-IN-PUBLICATION DATA

Dunn, Stephen, date.
  Local visitations : poems / by Stephen Dunn.— 1st ed.
      p. cm.
  ISBN 0-393-05200-1 (hardcover)
  I. Title.
  PS3554.U49 L59 2003
  811'.54—dc21

                                                    2002014204

W. W. Norton & Company, Inc., 500 Fifth Avenue, New York, N.Y. 10110
www.wwnorton.com

W. W. Norton & Company Ltd., Castle House, 75/76 Wells Street,
London W1T 3QT

  1 2 3 4 5 6 7 8 9 0

For Jonathan Holden

Contents

Here

Local Visitations

Acknowledgments

The American Poetry Review: "The Others," "The Arm"

The Georgia Review: "Charlotte Brontë in Leeds Point," "George Eliot in Beach Haven," "Tolstoy in South Jersey," "Twain in Atlantic City"

Margie: "Sisyphus Among Cold Dark Matter"

Michigan Quarterly: "Jane Austen in Egg Harbor," "Dostoyevsky in Wildwood"

New Delta Review: "From Nowhere"

Poetry: "Lewis Carroll in the Rabbit Hole," "Henry James in Cape May," "Flaubert in Smithville," "Mary Shelley in Brigantine," "Harriet Beecher Stowe in Sweetwater," "Melville at Barnegat Light," "Sisyphus's Acceptance," "Sisyphus and the Sudden Lightness," "Sisyphus in the Suburbs," "The Affair"

Quarterly West: "Goethe in Galloway Township," "Hawthorne in Tuckerton," "Stephen Crane in Longport"

Rattle: "The Crossing," "A Bowl of Fruit"

Shenandoah: "Circular," "Questions," "The Unsaid"

Southern Review: "Chekhov in Port Republic," "Dickens in Pleasantville," "Poe in Margate," "Stendhal in Sea Isle City"

Southern Humanities Review: "Flying Low"

Witness: "The Animals of America"

A group of these poems won The J. Howard and Barbara M. J. Wood Prize from *Poetry*.

With deep appreciation and gratitude to my important readers: Lawrence Raab, Philip Booth, Lois Dunn, Gregory Djanikian, Jonathan Aaron, BJ Ward, Carol Houck Smith, Sam Toperoff, Jack Driscoll, Kathleen Flenniken, Jill Rosser, and Peter Murphy, with a special loving bow to Barbara Hurd.

My indebtedness to James Hollis and his book *Creating a Life*, especially the passages about Sisyphus.

To pretend is to know oneself.

—*Fernando Pessoa*

When we had all the answers,
they changed the questions.

—*Eduardo Galeano*

Don't let it end like this. Tell them
I said something.

—*last words of Pancho Villa*

A Bowl of Fruit

> For me, the pleasure of poetry
> is taking it apart.
> —*Jeanne-Andrée Nelson*

Jeanne, I have spent days arranging
this bowl of fruit, all for you,
knowing how much you love fruit
(not to eat, of course, but to examine),
and I've been careful to make sure
the bananas are the shape of bananas,
that the oranges rhyme with oranges,
and for your pleasure I've included
a lone pear, which may signify
something to you I haven't intended,
which is my intention.
No doubt you've begun to question
why the quince and the apple
are so close together, and (knowing you)
if there might be a worm
in the apple, whether this gift
is a gift at all. And perhaps it's true
that I've covered up the worm hole
with putty, painted over it perfectly,
though this would be a mystery
that only can be solved
by cutting open or biting into,
letting the juices run down the sides
of your mouth, or onto your hands.
It would be the kind of bold probing
I would love for you to love, the final

messiness of theory, still life breaking open
into life, the discovery that the secret worm,
if real, will not permit you any distance.
But surely by now you've come to realize
there is no worm, only this bowl of fruit
made of words, only these seductions.

Sisyphus
and Other Poems

Circular

Daylight illuminated, but only for those
who had some knowing in their seeing,
and night fell for everyone, but harder
for some. A belief in happiness bred
despair, though despair could be assuaged
by belief, which required faith,
which made those who had it
one-eyed amid the beautiful contraries.
Love at noon that was still love at dusk
meant doubt had been subjugated
for exactly that long, and best to have music
to sweeten a sadness, underscore joy.
Those alone spoke to their dogs,
but also to plants, to the brilliant agreeableness
of air, while those together were left
to address the wall or open door of each other.
Oh for logs in the fireplace and a winter storm,
some said. Oh for scotch and a sitcom, said others.
Daylight concealed, but only for those
fond of the enormous puzzle, and night rose up
earth to sky, pagan and unknowable.
How we saw it was how it was.

Sisyphus's Acceptance

These days only he could see the rock,
so when he stopped for a bagel
at the bagel store, then for a newspaper
at one of those coin-operated stalls,
he looked like anyone else
on his way to work. Food—

the gods reasoned—
would keep him alive
to suffer, and news of the world
could only make him feel worse.
Let him think he has choices;
he belongs to us.

Rote not ritual, a repetition
which never would mean more
at the end than at the start . . .
Sisyphus pushed his rock
past the aromas of bright flowers,
through the bustling streets
into plenitude and vacuity,

every arrival the beginning
of a familiar descent. And sleep
was the cruelest respite;
at some murky bottom of himself
the usual muck rising up.

One morning, however, legs hurting,
the sun beating down,
again weighing the quick calm of suicide
against this punishment that passed for life,
Sisyphus smiled.

It was the way a gambler smiles
when he finally decides to fold
in order to stay alive
for another game, a smile
so inward it cannot be seen.

The gods sank back
in their airy chairs. Sisyphus sensed
he'd taken something from them,
more on his own than ever now.

Flying Low

For Jim Hollis

As creations go, I don't think the sky can be improved,
burnished silver, bluish pink, northern lights and storms,
its invitation to the universe, quantum and quark.
But here, just the old numinous beauty of fog,
the sun busting a gut behind it, morning coming on.

At the bottom of depression, says one James Hollis,
is some meaningful task waiting to be found.
Maybe I should butler someone other than myself
for a change, hire myself out, no charge.

As creations go, I could use some work.
For weeks now, black wings, black wings,
a wish to be undetectable and dangerous,
yet searched for just the same.

Soon, if history will out, the fog will turn
to low mist, cling to the fields and stunted pines.
If I were someone else I might walk to the end
of Chestnut Neck where the marshland begins.
But I'm flying low, thank you, right where I am.

Not far off: the tea-colored cranberry bogs, and all
the unseen indwellings of the smallest things.
Hollis used to live close by. It was back
when the ocean was more pure, and all of us
the more interesting for being on the verge.

The Others

The others have gone down to the dock
to watch the tall ships come in.
The others are sailing the ships.

Beauty has slipped her arm into theirs
as they explain the shipbuilder's art.
Blue is their sky, a good wind
that which comes up when they yearn

to join still others on an opposite shore.
It is not that they are better dressed,
it's how their bodies tack and carry.
It *is* that they are better dressed.

You have no interest in tall ships.
You don't know a spar from a bowsprit.
Elegance, for you, is an afterthought.

But the others are drinking now on their decks.
They are making love with other others
in the lower cabins.
They've draped their perfect clothes

over the portholes because they like the dark.
They're not trying to keep you out.
It's what you hate the most—
about you, not a single thought.

Sisyphus and the Sudden Lightness

It was as if he had wings, and the wind
behind him. Even uphill the rock
seemed to move of its own accord.

Every road felt like a shortcut.

Sisyphus, of course, was worried;
he'd come to depend on his burden,
wasn't sure who he was without it.

His hands free, he peeled an orange.
He stopped to pet a dog.
Yet he kept going forward, afraid
of the consequences of standing still.

He no longer felt inclined to smile.

It was then that Sisyphus realized
the gods must be gone, that his wings
were nothing more than a perception
of their absence.

He dared to raise his fist to the sky.
Nothing, gloriously, happened.

Then a different terror overtook him.

From Nowhere

From nowhere in almost no time
came a fish that needed to fly
came the edifice after the cave
came the tulip and the Dutch,
the order of which I'm not sure
Came the burro, came the zebra
amazement before the telescope
what needed to be screwed
before the screw
Came the cockroach and the scarab
the auk and the ape
Came music and the savage heart,
the soothing of which is unproved
Came armor after the wound
love after it became easier to survive
came fickleness, came betrayal
after a second one walked by
Came the bat before radar
came the spider, came the loom
Came the hat and the hatrack
the mastodon and the spoon,
the order, I'm afraid,
once again wrong
In hardly any time at all
came language, came the lie

came neuroses after leisure
surely the motel after the car
Came *now*, that chameleon,
unseeable until it moved

The Other Side of Time

is where they reside, those not yet born,
unaware that some deep thrust
and low sigh might send them tumbling
into the sorrows of experience.

It cannot be said that they have minds.
All around them, circles, ellipses, vibrations,
as if the empty landscape
were gathering itself, about to bloom.

Night is the name of their day,
all phenomena interchangeable.
Far off, an occasional galaxy on fire—
the unborn never troubled.

Moral and immoral don't exist
where they are.
But a thousand mistakes await them.
Desire will soon torque and uncalm.

They'll have begun the long forgetting
of that time when everything felt possible.
When there were no reasons to hesitate.
When life just called and they came.

Sisyphus Among Cold Dark Matter

> Cold dark matter betrays its presence
> only by the gravitational pull it exerts
> on the shapes and movements of galaxies.
>   — *The Atlantic City Press*

He walked out of his house thinking that wherever he walked
he'd be in it. On the rickety bridge into town,
under the portentous slate-gray sky, especially behind the faces
of people, he sensed something seminal and hidden,
if not cold dark matter itself, perhaps the very something a soul
could siphon for nourishment, a typically famished soul.

Even indoors, in the Grand Union's antiseptic aisles,
then at the outlet amid discarded hand-me-downs,
and later at Faye's place, menu in hand, he was sure
massive weakly interacting particles led their invisible lives.
Yet he knew he was no galaxy, no matter
what dark pull he felt, or the size of his needs.

But this day he couldn't stop feeling the universe
was nearby, in the smallest things.
When the waitress at Faye's asked if everything was all right,
he said Yes, yet felt an immensity to her question,
understood Yes to be the lie we tell so we can continue on,
a kind of nourishment of its own. He tipped her well,
wondering if anyone could more than glimpse another's hell.

Knowledge

Some things like stones yield
only their opacity,
remain inscrutably themselves.
To the trained eye they offer their age,
some small planetary news.

Which suggests the world
becomes more mysterious, not less,
the more we know.

God knows is how we begin a sentence
when we refuse to acknowledge what we know.

Gravitas is what Newton must have felt
when gravity became clear to him.

Presto, said the clown as he pulled
a quarter from behind my ear
when I was five. The very same ear in fact
that pressed itself to a snail's vacant house
and found an ocean.

The problem is how to look intelligent
with our mouths agape,
how to be delighted, not stupefied
when the caterpillar shrugs
and becomes a butterfly.

It's on a clear surface we can best see
the signs point many ways.

God knows nothing we don't know.
We gave him every word he ever said.

Angels in the Rafters, Bats in Heaven

A Love Poem

If it were so, there'd be angel-fear, bat-worship,
and angels coming too close would be whacked
with tennis rackets, poisoned in attics.
Bats would be silly, black wish fulfillments,
or our better natures with wings, often elsewhere,
come from far away to help.

In other words, my dear, nothing in the world
would change and we'd still be faced
with how to reconcile the insistence of laundry
and the need to pay bills
with the fragility of our yearnings,
how to love each other amid the encroachments.

Of course, such reversals could persist,
the agitation of crows outside our window
reminding us that bats are always nearby
sensed but not seen, or that an angel
in daylight might be rabid, a danger to us all.
What would we do then? The imagination
suddenly more sovereign than we ever intended,
gone the useful restrictions, the holding in.

Sisyphus at Rest

A small L-shaped apartment. No evidence
of comfort anywhere, unless stillness itself
is comfort. Even the bed looks spartan,
without give, its one pillow like wood.

Books, scraps of notes strewn on the floor
to either side of his hardbacked chair.
The faucets drip,
the dirty dishes have grown mold.

At the first aluminum glow of dawn
he wakes to watch its slow surge
give way to isolated lights in kitchens
in buildings like his, the streets stirring

with workers and shadows and cars.
Sisyphus has settled in to write
about how it was out there, and what
it feels like to be shuck of it, alone.

On one scrap, "I was good all day
and did the things I was supposed to do."
On another, "How boring sorrows are."
Already he can recognize a tendency

to up the voltage when he has little to say,
to smokescreen the insignificant
with an abracadabra of big words.
And sometimes he can hear a false music

behind something he's said in earnest.
Meanwhile there is such a meanwhile!
He dreams of women, the lure and unfairness
of their beauty. He dreams

of a gate opening in a distant field.
But more often he finds himself dreaming
of his rock, wishing it back, the better
to defend himself against so many hours.

Late afternoons the liquor cabinet
has begun to call him from across the room.
He showers then, slathers his cock with soap

and goes to town. He waits for the sweet,
forgiving cocoon of dusk to surround.
It does. Every day. Every day without fail.

The Crossing

You will soon be crossing the great waters,
the captain said, and there was a broken violin
behind him, and a harp that played by itself.
You will soon be crossing the great waters,
he repeated, and it will forever be too late
no matter what time it is.
This followed by a familiar hush of importance.
I was both the dreamer and director of a dream,
that much was clear, and I was the captain, too.
I felt no fear. In the distance a stage-set sea.
When the captain said, Self-consciousness
is your life raft, you must leave it behind,
I suddenly wanted to protest but couldn't
form the words, my mouth a cartoon
of a mouth agape, frozen in impotence,
a bubble of silence issuing from it.
Then we were setting out, the captain
and I, into the vast expanse on a windless day,
sharks all around with their broad smiles
and every scud in the sky a face from my past.

The Animals of America

The animals have come down from the hills
and through the forests and across the prairies.
They are American animals, and carry with them
a history of their slaughter. There's not one
who doesn't sleep with an eye open.

Out of necessity the small have banded
with the large, the large with the large
of different species. When dark comes
they form an enormous circle.

It's all, after years of night-whispers
and long-range cries, coming together.

To make a new world the American animals
know there must be sacrifices. Every evening
a prayer is said for the spies who've volunteered
to be petted in the houses of the enemy.
"They are savages," one reported,
"let no one be fooled by their capacity for loving."

Sisyphus in the Suburbs

It was late and wine had wet
an aridity he'd forgotten he had.
He could feel the evening
arching above the house,
a good black dome. No ledges,
he realized, tempted him.
The once-inviting abyss
was now just a view.

Sisyphus put another CD on
and stroked the cat.
His wife was in Bermuda
with her younger sister,
celebrating the death
of winter, and a debt paid.
He missed her, and he did not.

He'd been mixing Janis Joplin
with Brahms, accountable now
to no one. The lights
from some long-desired festival
were not calling him.
No silent dog or calm ocean
made him fear the next moment.

But Sisyphus was amazed
how age sets in, how it just came
one day and stayed. And how far
away the past gets. His break
from the gods, just an episode now.

Tomorrow he'd brave the cold,
spireless mall, look for a gift.
He'd walk through the unappeasable
crowds as if some right thing
were findable and might be bestowed.

Here

The Arm

A doll's pink, broken-off arm
was floating in a pond
a man had come to with his dog.
The arm had no sad child nearby
to say it was hers, no parent to rescue it
with a stick or branch,

and this pleased the man to whom
absence always felt like opportunity.
He imagined a girl furious
at her younger sister, taking it out on her
one limb at a time.

Yet the sun was glancing off
the arm's little pink fingers,
and the pond's heart-shaped lily pads
seemed to accentuate an oddness,
which he thought beautiful.

When he and the dog looked for
the doll's body but couldn't find it,
a different image came to him,
of a father who hated the fact
that his son liked dolls.
What was floating there

was a punishment that didn't work,
for the boy had come to love
his one-armed doll even more.
Once again the man was struck
by how much misery
the human spirit can absorb.

His dog wanted to move on,
enough of this already.
But the man was creating little waves
with his hands, and the arm, this thing
his wife was sure to question,
was slowly bobbing toward him.

The Unsaid

One night they both needed different things
of a similar kind; she, solace; he, to be consoled.
So after a wine-deepened dinner
when they arrived at their house separately
in the same car, each already had been failing
the other with what seemed
an unbearable delay of what felt due.
What solace meant to her was being understood
so well you'd give it to her before she asked.
To him, consolation was a network
of agreements: say what you will
as long as you acknowledge what I mean.
In the bedroom they undressed and dressed
and got into bed. The silence was what fills
a tunnel after a locomotive passes through.
Days later the one most needy finally spoke.
"What's on TV tonight?" he said this time,
and she answered, and they were okay again.
Each, forever, would remember the failure
to give solace, the failure to be consoled.
And many, many future nights
would find them turning to their respective sides
of the bed, terribly awake and twisting up
the covers, or, just as likely, moving closer
and sleeping forgetfully the night long.

The Affair

Just when it seemed his marriage had settled
into sleepy comforts and an occasional boost
from a blue pill, he learned what the luckiest
of adulterers come to know: you don't need
some large dissatisfaction to motivate
an affair, some overarching complaint.
A door would open in a faraway city;
inside, everything felt like its own good reason.
Of course, the lying unnerved and diminished him,
but after a while it felt strangely humane,
better, he told himself, for all concerned.
He took pride that he gave his divided attention
wholly to whomever he was with.
His wife was his better half by more than half.
His lover was the everything
he allowed himself partially to have.
When their sex turned into love
adultery suddenly felt wrong—the word,
he wanted another word for what they did.
And there were the bones of his marriage
in plain sight, meat on them still.
For a moment he longed for the old days
when there were gods to take offense,
when a man who wanted too much

would be reduced to size
with a life-long redundancy or thunderbolt.
But, no, there'd be nothing so neat.
It came to a choice, and he chose everything.
He left almost everything behind.

Questions

If on a summer afternoon a man should find himself
in love with only one woman
in a sea of women, all the others mere half-naked
swimmers and floaters, and if that one woman
therefore is clad in radiance
while the mere others are burdened by their bikinis,
then what does he do with a world
suddenly so small, the once unbiased sun
shining solely on her? And if that afternoon
turns dark, fat clouds like critics dampening
the already wet sea, does the man run—
as he normally would—for cover, or does he dive
deeper in, get so wet he is beyond wetness
in an underworld utterly hers? And when
he comes up for air, as he must,
when he dries off and dresses up, as he must,
how will the pedestrian streets feel?
What will the street lamps illuminate? How exactly
will he hold her so that everyone can see
she doesn't belong to him, and he won't let go?

A New Year

It begins again and always—in this part
of the stunned and stunning world—
in winter. Thus, without birdsong,

without any hopeful yellow flower
in sight, we make our noise,
we kiss the one we came with,

then look for others,
happy, for the moment, to have an excuse.
There's no one, we realize, but us

to sweeten the day, lessen the viciousness,
which is reason enough to drink
ourselves brave. It's time to resolve

to do something about which
we have little resolve, time to dance
and forget in order to dance again.

Time itself has made its steady way down.
We witnessed it, commonplace
these days as fallen gods.

What can startle us now? A new thing
comes; it takes its place among
the microchips and distant wars.

Here you are, new thing, you
enormous you. I've cleared my calendar.
Once you arrived, I had no choice.

She

She loved white lilies and a good rain.
About such, she was of the many.
But she preferred swamps to the postcards
lakes could be,
the word chardonnay, just slightly,
to the actual taste of it.
In this way she permitted you
to fall in love with her. Because she
wasn't lost, she couldn't be found
in her quietness. If you had to ask
you didn't know, her smile said.
Steady needed to be your unsteadiness
in her presence. She gathered eel grass
and traced the leavings of black bears.
She slid through small openings in caves,
bringing with her her own light.
She didn't expect you to follow.
To truly follow her was to wait
until she wrote it down, until she herself
knew where she'd been.
That's when you'd first meet her
again and again, on the page,
where she belonged to everyone.

But only you (and the several before you)
knew that she loved
afternoon naps and long awakenings.

For Barbara

Best

Best to have a partner whose desire matches yours
so you each feel there's no time
to pull back the covers, your respective clothes
Pollocking the floor, perhaps the beautiful accident
of her bra commingling with your sock on a bedpost,
and just a stain or two to prove nothing like this
could ever be immaculate, Jesus Christ having come
involuntarily from your lips, Oh Jesus Christ,
all four of the hospital corners intact
in what has been without doubt an emergency room,
both of you having died and gone to heaven
and now, amazingly, breathing evenly once again.

Often the Pleasures of Departure

Often the pleasures of departure are so close
to the genuine sadness of leaving
he feared his goodbyes

would reveal it, an errant tone perhaps
at odds with a sincere word.
And though he knew that anyone's heart

might lean two ways at once,
he also knew that no one could be comfortable
with such a truth, not even himself.

"I'll be thinking of you," he'd say at the door,
while already he'd be in his car,
singing, the music all the way up.

It wasn't necessarily that he'd be going
to someone else; it simply could be
the relief of farting a great private fart,

or that aloneness itself was his mistress.
When he'd call from another city,
scotch-high or merely sleepy,

he always wished it were possible to say—
for truth's sake and because he felt it
a lot—"I miss you a little."

Here

Maybe this world
is another planet's Hell.
        —*Aldous Huxley*

Sometimes it feels otherworldly, what I've felt,
my heart residing in its own peculiar dark,
or suddenly aglow, lit up from within.
I sense then I'm on one of the good planets

where mistakes and wild, venal joys
lead to ordinary suffering, not banishment or doom.
Whatever we must endure,
doesn't it take place closer to home?

I know how I feel about murderers or men
with lollipops who lead children into the woods.
Still, eternal damnation doesn't do
anyone any good. Most of us pay now

for what we do and have done, or slide
like the poor and the helpless toward
the slammed gavel of a fate. That's enough, I say
out loud to no one in any world. Yet here

and there, though mostly here, even fate is reversible
with struggle or luck. More than once I've walked
under the sun and beneath the luminous moon
not knowing what or whom to thank.

Local
Visitations

The Great 19th Century Writers

The Resurrections

Because the famous usually have little to say
to each other after the first paeans of praise,
the poet thought that for their own sakes
he'd have them live in separate towns.
They'd be invisible as Bellow or Roth

would be on any New Jersey street.
Beyond ambition now, they'd have some peace.
But what peace for the attentive?
Maybe they'd live as they once had,
noticing everything while choosing little,

seeking answers, distrusting them, inventing
what came next. Maybe each day they'd take on
more and more properties of flesh,
wishing to have something to renounce.
He hated to admit it, but the great 19th century

novelists and storytellers had given him more
rare glimpses into the cohabitation of the mysterious
and the real, more hard news from the mind's
hidden caves and provinces, than had the poets
of the same period. Sure, there were the Dickinsons

and Baudelaires, the Hopkinses, the Blakes.
But novelists were less likely to publicly brood,
or stink up a community because of their friendships
with the abyss. Were much more likely to dwell
in actual towns with actual barber shops and guilt.

Whereas the poets offered those endless physical emblems
of the soul, and entrees into parallel universes
populated by people who never had to wash or do chores.
Sure, one could think, say, of Pushkin or Whitman
as exceptions, their attention to little lives, grass, slime.

But Plato was right, so difficult to govern with poets around.
South Jersey could easily become a region doomed
to drift into decade after decade speaking the unspoken.
No, only the storytellers would be rescued from fame's stasis.
Choices had to be made. And there'd be rules.

Chekhov in Port Republic

No one but me took special notice of his presence,
and he hadn't come to heal, unless to render
the residual sorrow behind all our pretensions
is to heal. He was as attentive to torpor
as he was to vitality, and he knew
how pretty words and big promises could swindle,
not unlike how the church fools the poor.

Some of us had seen his black satchel, had heard
he'd helped the Jenkins woman late one night
when, bruised and bleeding, she knocked on his door.
In the old country many men beat their wives,
blaming it on vodka or weather. He didn't believe
geography made much difference; we were all the same.
And he, well, he was in the business of making things

imperishable, and none of us, finally, could be saved.
He'd said the best stories require a cold eye,
his fellow humans frozen in the folly of being themselves.
But of course he tended to her wounds.
Bandages were what a doctor used. The writer
in him wanted the world made visible, exposed.

He'd taken the Olsen house set back off Chestnut.
Now and then a lady with a dog would be seen
in the driveway, though it was presumed he lived alone.
Neatly trimmed beard, eyes that seemed to forgive
even as they pierced, he resembled his photographs

before he got sick. I had no trouble believing the dead
travel between two worlds, like minds, like wind.
Something in me must have needed him here.
These would be the years (I'd see to it) his early death
deprived him of, Chekhov Chekhov once again,
the self-satisfied among us, the smug, laid bare.

Charlotte Brontë in Leeds Point

From her window marshland stretched for miles.
If not for egrets and gulls, it reminded her of the moors
behind the parsonage, how the fog often hovered
and descended as if sheltering some sweet compulsion
the age was not ready to see. On clear days the jagged
skyline of Atlantic City was visible—Atlantic City,
where all compulsions had a home.

"Everything's too easy now," she said to her neighbor,
"nothing resisted, nothing gained." Once, at eighteen,
she dreamed of London's proud salons glowing
with brilliant fires and dazzling chandeliers.
Already her own person—passionate, assertive—
soon she'd create a governess insistent on rights equal
to those above her rank. "The dangerous picture

of a natural heart," one offended critic carped.
She'd failed, he said, to let religion reign
over the passions and, worse, she was a woman.
Now she was amazed at what women had,
doubly amazed at what they didn't.
But she hadn't come back to complain or haunt.
Her house on the bay was modest, adequate.

It need not accommodate brilliant sisters
or dissolute brothers, spirits lost or fallen.
Feminists would pay homage, praise her honesty
and courage. Rarely was she pleased. After all,
she was an artist; to speak of honesty in art,
she knew, was somewhat beside the point.
And she had married, had even learned to respect

the weakness in men, those qualities they called
their strengths. Whatever the struggle, she wanted men
included. Charlotte missed reading chapters to Emily,
Emily reading chapters to her. As ever, though, she'd try
to convert present into presence, something unsung
sung, some uprush of desire frankly acknowledged,
even in this, her new excuse for a body.

Dickens in Pleasantville

It is neither the best nor worst of times,
no children begging in the streets, or fathers
coming home coughing, covered with soot.
The mills, mines, and factories
are the nearby casino hotels, all in one,
and Dickens sees in the workers' eyes

a familiar dulling of the spirit. But they have jobs.
In their small, frame houses they have everything
debt can buy. He'll be The Ghost of Promises
Made and Promises Broken. He'll try
to figure out why the American poor
aspire to be like their oppressors.

Dickens on Main Street, admiring the new
streetlights. Dickens at the Pleasantville Mall
as if stumbling into one of the country's cathedrals.
Dickens at the Middle School thinking of his knuckles
being rapped, a cane leaving marks on his bottom.
He writes in his journal: "It's not a disorder

but an order that is horrible." He sees someone
he might call a Heep, then a Pecksniff, looks for
anyone who might be doing some far better thing.
Dickens is moved by what the children know
and cannot change, their parents working graveshifts
and second jobs, all the normal difficulties of love.

Yet he is just learning what a ghost can
and cannot do. Someone is controlling him, he feels,
figuring it out as he goes, and for the first time
Dickens understands the limitations of being
a mere character. He wants to say something harsh
to the person in charge. But he's not given the words.

Poe in Margate

To come back and learn his alcoholism
was an illness—Poe had to laugh at that.
He knew the vanity of excuses better than anyone,
and how good self-destruction feels when one
is in the act of it. Still, he thought, you must be sober
to write your autobiography, set things straight.

He'd give up all notions of a kingdom by the sea,
try to see things as they were and are.
But soon came the old, constant rebellion
of the senses and mind, soon he remembered
that truth was an enormous house shrouded in mist
with many secret vaults, and that perfect sobriety

is the state in which you make the version of yourself
you like best, just another way to lie. He'd have
just one drink before dinner to ease in the night,
and from his window watch monstrous Lucy the Elephant
closing up, tourists no longer walking in her body
and looking out of her eyes. The world was stranger

than he had imagined it, certainly no less strange.
The newspaper that arrived daily at his doorstep
was storied with men who murdered because voices
told them to, girls who killed their newborns
then returned to the prom. In his autobiography
he'd insist on the ultimate sanity of the artist,

regardless of what he did with his life. He'd tell
of his long hours of calculation and care,
how when Usher's house fell into that tarn
it was a victory of precision over the loose ends
of a troubled mind, how his insane narrators needed
everything that was rational in him all of the time.

Jane Austen in Egg Harbor

In search of the right place she'd taken the local
that makes its way through South Jersey towns,
twenty or so passengers aboard in motley dress,
all minding their different manners. A small train,
just two cars, one class, *carrying many classes*,
she mused, ever the anthropologist.

And she thought of extravagance and self-denial,
her twin seductions, so hard to measure now—
the familiar boundaries of her vanished century
long gone. But as usual she found herself poised
between them, keen-eyed, looking in and looking out.
(Advocacy: a clear indicator to her of a lesser mind.)

It was twilight when she arrived, the outdoor platform
gray, the air cool. From the station she could see
the lights of town, little else, and walked across the street
toward them. Egg Harbor, White Horse Pike,
delicious words! Her suitcase weighed almost nothing,
as if she'd packed only for the demands of the soul.

Long modest dress and hand-knit shawl—she looked
strangely formal. Someone whistled from a car.
All contempt, she thought, is self-contempt,
and kept walking. It was a common mistake
to think her shockable because demure. She liked
that the main street wasn't called Main Street,

liked the great width of it, how the unfancy cars
were parked diagonally. And the neighborhood, well,
felt neighborly, which meant to her full of drama
and high intrigue. She'd learn the nuances soon,
maybe start a book club, everyone reading out loud
before getting down to the gossip only fools don't love.
She thought she might be happy here.

Flaubert in Smithville

There wasn't a single landscape he longed for.
Neither mountains nor meadows interested him,
and cities, no matter how abuzz with commerce,
were just there waiting for someone to write them,
just more evidence of a benumbed, unborn world.

Smithville, with its knick-knack shops, faux
Colonial village, busloads of retirees,
was as good a place as any to stay in one's room.
In the town itself he could see the bare outline
of a form. He who once said, "Be regular and orderly

in your daily life so you can be violent and original
in your work," arranged the pencils on his desk, tidied
the table where his books were strewn.
He wrote to his beloved: "A good day. A few sentences.
One that almost has the feel of the true."

He sent out for pizza, for Chinese. Now and then
he'd venture into the streets to hear the language,
its tics and nasal music, where the silences fell.
Smithville's quaintness was never more aggressive
than when he observed it, jotted it down.

Could a good writer use "condo" in a sentence?
Or must it be spoken by a character, a vulgarian
perhaps, or perhaps the politest man in town?
He worried about this an entire afternoon.
Only Emma, his neighbor, had seen his immaculate

study, his kitchen with a kettle and little more.
Her husband had treated Flaubert's flu,
and she came by a few times to discuss the novels
she had read. He let her in as if into a laboratory,
and listened as she floated between things dreamed

and things that could have been. In his notebook:
"A pretty woman with men problems keeps annoying me,
but I think I can use her and make her die."
Flaubert was always excited when she left, which meant
he felt a desire to invent. Himself he'd hide.

Henry James in Cape May

Though the society he sought did not exist here,
no coteries of fine talk or drawing rooms
where the posturings of the privileged could be skewered,
he nevertheless took pleasure in the Victorian B&B's,
and the old, grand mansions that lined the shore.

Now in a rocker on the balcony of one of them,
the many-dormered Angel by the Sea,
he pondered the ghastliness that all immortals
were unable to die—days like this, years,
in which landscape and one's mind never changed.

Yet he'd always be the central consciousness
of wherever he was, and he trusted, inevitably,
that there'd be some Daisy or Isabel
with whom to dine, then to send out into
the common vagaries of the Cape May night.

The author as pimp, in it to plumb a discrepancy,
to watch, perhaps, one of his ladies
sit down at the wrong table, attempt to speak French
to a bunch of ruffians, say, from Rahway,
or perhaps mistake a mistress for a wife.

He'd be content to have observed for us a small
human tendency, one of the laws of the heart.
Then, for him, a Courvoisier, a good night's rest,
and a sentence that wouldn't stop, modifier
after modifier, turns, hesitations, refinements.

But was he worrying now that someone who thought
and couldn't stop thinking may never have loved?
And were we who watched him there watching us
so unfair, so spoiled, to regret that one who gave us
something had also not given us something else?

George Eliot in Beach Haven

She was not one to expect that after death
there'd be balm or bliss, so when she felt
a cool soothing wind blow over her
and her windows were closed,
she wanted to protest.
Which was the last thing she recalled.

How many years had passed? Here she was
on the main drag in Beach Haven, a summer's night,
listening to a girl with a nose ring and tongue stud
speaking to a similarly bejewled boy.
Was this death? Some kind of cosmic joke?
There wasn't an adult in sight.

In her time, she had asked, What can a woman *do*
in life? This was after she left the church, took up
with a married man, became an unacceptable guest
almost everywhere. But brilliant men sought her
brilliant company. In her blue velvet dress
she out-talked Darwin and Dickens.

Marian Evans? Mary Ann Cross? If she were
to make herself known, she'd use one of those names.
George Eliot never died. It was she who had.
And it seemed now that a woman could be direct,
could offer A Study of Provincial Life
and need no disguise, maybe even flaunt herself.

Was this tongue-studded girl some modern version
of the radical she'd been, a new kind of exile?
Listening to her, it was hard to believe
the girl had read Rousseau or anyone.
But this was America. How was one to tell?
Already she'd heard the word "awesome" twice,

yet no one present seemed stunned or transformed,
everyone in perfect agreement. Where was the fun
of saying one thing and meaning another?
Suddenly George Eliot felt an old desire to conceal.
A woman with a past, she decided, always wears a mask.
She can't help it, and it becomes her.

Tolstoy in South Jersey

No matter where Tolstoy was placed he'd bolt,
one day from New Gretna, next from Blue Anchor
many miles west. The man couldn't be contained.
There he'd be in blueberry fields talking to workers,
then at the cranberry bogs deep in the Barrens.

The sex shops that dotted Route 30 repelled, lured,
finally bored him. Epitaphs on headstones
interested him more, imagining the Colonial past,
lovers and loved ones, the battles, successes,
suicides. He canoed the Mullica, took in the odors

of lilac and lily, noted the shreds of light
coming through the branches of leafy oaks.
South Jersey, he discovered, was a realm
of the yet-to-be-created, a panorama of nameless
names, its people asprawl, their kindness, malice,

beauty, sweat of industry, drowsiness of ambition,
awaiting their approximate, never final nouns.
All he needed, he said, was a year, maybe two,
and he'd deliver it, clock it, make it as real as Moscow
in flames, the harsh countryside covered with snow.

Stephen Crane in Longport

Occasionally the weak survive
because the god that doesn't exist
wants to give us something to misinterpret.
That's what Crane was thinking

as he washed up on Longport beach.
He seemed to remember the afterlife
had been a boat forever lost
in the doldrums of the sea. Then a storm,

the boat's captain thrown overboard,
suddenly captain of nothing,
waves buffeting him and his crew
until they surrendered and went under.

He saw a man, suntanned, hairy-chested,
squatting near a dune, eating something
he'd pulled from a bag. It was
(by the expression on the man's face) bitter,

though the man kept on eating
as if he couldn't get enough. Crane felt
he was dreaming a writer's dream; he'd arrived
in a world he himself had made.

By this time many people from town
were making their way toward him.
No, they walked right by
as if they were pursuing the horizon.

It's pointless, Crane wanted to say,
wherever you're all going.
But he knew they'd think he was lying,
or maybe not even hear him.

Stendhal in Sea Isle City

Because he believed "Everything can be acquired in solitude
except character" (and his character was fully formed),
he thought a beach town in winter would suit him. Just a house
with a good view removed from the populace's windy nothings.
He'd start another memoir about Napoleon. But Stendhal

had been dead for so long he'd forgotten how one's body
tends to confound one's epigrams. He loved women. They,
not character building, had always been for him
the main reason to mingle. The local Weekly was pleased
when he volunteered to write a column "About Love."

It was an old tactic of his and others: to let their writing flirt
for them. He wrote charmingly about his weariness with virtue
in hopes some like-minded Héloise would see it.
In one column he asked, "Has six months of your life
ever been made miserable by love?" Héloises up and down

the coast responded with scented stationary and their numbers.
For Stendhal, it was life after death all over again.
Every week he upped the ante, inviting the anger of women
he wasn't interested in. He insisted on the pleasures

of what he called a tender dominance. He spoke of the secret
wish of even the strongest woman to wholly yield.

"Read me," he'd say in a whisper over the phone, "and it will
make you suspect there's a kind of happiness you've never known."

Twain in Atlantic City

For a man who'd been everywhere, from Hannibal
westward, south down the Mississippi, to as far east
as Europe, who'd known stagecoach, steamboat,
raft, railroad, now to find himself among glitter
and ruin seemed just one more stop on a path
crooked as life itself. He hadn't yet learned where it led.
Perhaps, he thought, it's what couldn't be known.

In the Inlet, amid Hispanics and blacks,
he felt like an old white man in a white suit.
(Like the others, he'd come back looking like
his last famous photograph.) But the residents
had their own concerns, hardly looked his way.
Always flush with money or fresh out of it,
he liked to gamble at the Showboat, sometimes the Taj.

Where better to see versions of the King and the Duke,
and hundreds of Widow Douglases playing the slots?
Our pretenses, gaucheries, our bouts with conscience—
Twain walked through the city with a smile on his face.
Life on the Atlantic, he could have titled it.
The raucous Clemens still was fused with the wry,
yet outraged Twain. One day he'd investigate Park Place,

the next see what pleasures there were on Kentucky,
already having noted the damage that stretched
from Virginia to New York. He'd known since childhood
that nice people have nasty minds. And because he knew
the fake in himself, he could spot a fake across any room—
some posture, some inner rigging full of thin air.
No American was safe anywhere, especially here.

Goethe in Galloway Township

Already it's clear by Goethe's silence that he's upset—
the lyric poet, critic, lover, botanist, philosopher,
novelist—reduced to just his name.
Most of the day he sketches—studies of the body—
amazing acts of memory, eerily precise.
He reads himself to sleep. Has no desire to go out.

Galloway Township is as unaware of him as it is
amorphous—swatches of farms and housing developments,
its people hard working, too practical to leverage their lives
for any absolute, unlike his Faust. He has gravitated
to Leipzig just off Duerer, a three-story house
not visible from the road, a broken swing in the yard.

It was pure selfishness to resurrect him, this man
who'd led such a full, long life. He'd learned to live
with pleasure's ache, intimacy's concealments, the strange
emptiness of achievement. Such men meet death
with equanimity, perhaps desiring only a little more light.
He's thinking: *Oblivion was such a better place
than this, I want to go back*. But it's too late for that.

Harriet Beecher Stowe in Sweetwater

> So you're the little woman who wrote
> the book that started this great war.
> —*Abraham Lincoln*

It wasn't exactly freedom that she felt
when she found herself on this northern lip
of the Mullica, a woman who somehow had gotten
to the other side. More like amazement,
and then the kind of loneliness the suddenly alive
experience when they realize
no one else can know what they've known.

Birds were twittering. A strong wind
ruffled the maples. The sun glinted
off the water like . . . sun glinting off water.
She couldn't think of a single comparison,
but such felicities didn't matter now.
A sadness rising. An occlusion of the heart.
Hard for her to feel good when so many others

didn't make it, forever left behind. Yet she
was no Eliza; no slave-catchers were in hot pursuit.
Just her and a foreign landscape.
Shouldn't be difficult, she thought, for a white person
to settle in, be accommodated, accommodate.
It would be months before she'd discover
some descendants of slaves disapproved of her book,

resented the way she handled Tom. A *Tom*, an epithet.
How that hurt her. The friendly librarian advised
which critics to stay away from, which to read.
She read them all, found one statement she loved:
"It is the voices of women that shame us." And Lincoln's,
which brought back memories of the day he said it,
that tall man. Again, she didn't know what to feel.

Lewis Carroll in the Rabbit Hole

Too cruel, the poet thought, to bring Charles Dodgson back.
Let Lewis Carroll survive with *Wonderland* and *Looking-Glass*,
those romps through the indignities of childhood. Let's just think
of the Cheshire Cat, of croquet and the delightful violence
of using hedgehogs for balls, flamingos for mallets.

He was courtly, an Oxford Don, one of the great photographers
of his century. Should it matter that children were his only subjects,
young girls, some nude, and all of them his most important friends?
He'd pay for that in Pomona or Absecon, in any small town.

Or worse, be drawn in the evenings, if not all day, to the Internet,
titillated into finally acting out what must have been his dreams.
And wouldn't he be forced into therapy, shrunk and otherwise
reduced, thrust into the aridities of an examined life?

Yet the poet wanted him back, so much wanted to have him nearby,
this man who made the Snark and Jabberwock, who'd liberated
children's books from moralists. Every day for days the poet weighed
the frabjous, delicate goods and bads of Dodgson's return,
then with great sadness turned him away for good.

Dostoyevsky in Wildwood

Something about the edgy prospect of living alone
among small-time revelers and the honest escapes
of families from their poverty of routine,
something about the big, bedecked houses
not far from the cheap, inland bungalows—

a certain czarist grandeur and a desperate making do—
made Wildwood seem familiar. Here he was again,
old transformer armed with pen and paper
amid a populace. So what if he couldn't breathe
his native air; he'd always felt like a stranger.

He liked the ocean but hated the beach,
loved people more than he did
a single woman or man. Everywhere, though,
women in bikinis, women in shorts so short
you could follow a leg to some hidden center

of a rumored universe. What was a novelist to do
but worry about their souls? What was a man
to do but become an intoxicant? In one day
he'd seen more flesh than had his century.
But he was Dostoyevsky; he expected to be pulled

one way, then another. Wasn't the unbearable
one of his subjects? Wasn't the trick to yield to it
as if it weren't just *his* dilemma? Lord, he said to himself,
Let me for once not find myself everywhere I look.
Lord, let not the past overwhelm me.

Nights, teenagers of all classes dressed against elegance,
prowled the boardwalk under vacant, star-dense skies.
Swagger and shyness, rejection, cruelty, innuendo—
the ancient dance remained the same, though music now
in the foreground, odd machines on shoulders and waists.

Few seemed troubled that this was a kind of unhappiness.
He'd be unable to sleep because of the din.
Half-awake, he'd stitch together narratives,
the very stuff of his day torqued toward consequence.
In the mornings fishermen would line the jetties,

the ocean wild or calm, monotonously mysterious,
solemn. Beyond the breakers, pleasure boats
would be looking for dolphins and whales,
which would rise from the deep like epiphanies—
for a moment, only for a moment sufficient.

Was God a metaphor, and, if so, of what?
Shouldn't this, he thought, be a topic on their televisions?
But he could see everyone on the beach
was on vacation, that each wished to escape
for a while, maybe forever, all the great questions.

His Grand Inquisitor had known that even the disorderly
want decisions made for them, that hardly anyone
wishes to be free. Christ, their savior, for their sake,
must be killed. Dostoyevsky didn't believe that,
only understood it, that's how good a writer he was.

Now the people were heading inland to the bars and cafes.
He felt the profound loneliness of one who believes
we must love one another no matter what. And he sensed
an old fraudulence, the autocrat in him wishing to lie down
with the lamb. He'd stay the summer, if he had a choice.

Mary Shelley in Brigantine

Because the ostracized experience the world
in ways peculiar to themselves, often seeing it
clearly yet with such anger and longing
that they sometimes enlarge what they see,
she at first saw Brigantine as a paradise for gulls.
She must be a sea creature washed ashore.

How startling, though, no one knew about her past,
the scandal with Percy, the tragic early deaths,
yet sad that her Frankenstein had become
just a name, like Dracula or Satan, something
that stood for a kind of scariness, good for a laugh.
She found herself welcome everywhere.

People would tell her about Brigantine Castle,
turned into a house of horror. They thought
she'd be pleased that her monster roamed
its dark corridors, making children scream.
They lamented the day it was razed.
Thus Mary Shelley found herself accepted

by those who had no monster in them—
the most frightening people alive, she thought.
Didn't they know Frankenstein had abandoned
his creation, set him loose without guidance
or a name? Didn't they know what it feels like
to be lost, freaky, forever seeking who you are?

She was amazed now that people believed
you could shop for everything you might need.
She loved that in the dunes you could almost hide.
At the computer store she asked an expert
if there was such a thing as too much knowledge,
or going too far? He directed her to a website

where he thought the answers were.
Yet Mary Shelley realized that the pain she felt
all her life was gone. Could her children, dead so young,
be alive somewhere, too? She couldn't know
that only her famous mother had such a chance.
She was almost ready to praise this awful world.

Hawthorne in Tuckerton

Like the other great ones he wouldn't vanish
into his own destiny, kept showing up
in different parts of America, small pious towns
like this one, wooded, where he trusted
that what thumped in the human heart
would manifest, make its old nightly rounds.

"Scratch an American," he was overheard saying
at the diner, "and you'll find a Puritan."
And one man nodded while another
in a John Deere cap swallowed hard,
changed the subject to the Phillies.
Hawthorne still loved the repressed, the avoided.

Nothing made him more alert than a large passion
twisted, coiled in the recesses of an innocent.
But something had changed.
People camped without fear in the piney forest,
were simply amused by tales of the Jersey Devil.
And Tuckerton now had its Seaport. Its Dimmesdales

and Rappacinis had a stake in the market.
Their daughters wore lipstick and openly danced
to loud music. Hawthorne began to feel like the ghost
he was. Grace, he lamented, was once so poignant
before this democratization of the sacred. Adultery
so much more interesting when everyone didn't commit it.

Melville at Barnegat Light

If only families could make their way
through the ether that separates
the ever-existent from the dead-and-gone,
he would have brought his family with him.
But families of the famous leave nothing
visible behind them, thus are denied
future lives. Even in death life was unfair.

Melville had known the loneliness of the sea,
months of men enduring men, the terrible
singlemindedness that comes from long nights
in your cabin with a dream. He wanted no more
of it, but here in his blue Cape Cod, two blocks
from the lighthouse, it was just himself again,
finally well-known, and no one in whom

to confide the startling emptiness of success.
Evenings he thought he could hear sounds
of life from distant and disappearing shores.
Some mornings above the steel-gray sea
the light seemed purer than ever.
Must be the lucidity, he decided, that comes when sex
no longer distracts. Must be the journey's end.

When journalists called, asking if he would permit
an interview, he'd say he preferred not to.
When asked why, he preferred not to say.
No one wanted to hear—he was sure of it—
that for every magnitude he felt an incompleteness,
for every *Moby-Dick* or *Billy Budd* he could see
thousands of words unwritten, falterings of courage.

"There goes Melville," townspeople would say, proud
that a man whose books had been made into movies
walked among them. And he, who had called for
"The sane madness of vital truth," would tip his Greek
sailor's cap and smile. On this earth, he thought,
surely there must be some vista from which all of this
would make sense, surely some final gladdening.